Torremolinos, Fuengirola & Benalmadena Travel Guide

Attractions, Eating, Drinking, Shopping & Places To Stay

Sophie Bell

Table of Contents

Torremolinos

Previously just a sleepy fishing village on the outskirts of Malaga, Torremolinos is today anything but its turn-of-the-20th-century self. A popular escape for travellers from all corners of Europe, it is one of the Spanish Costa del Sol's most popular cities.

Although likely inhabited as early as the Neolithic Age, no other population has left as distinct a mark on Torremolinos as the Moors. Being skilled builders with particular affinity to using water as their aide, they harnessed the power of the stream that flowed to the coast from Los Manantiales and constructed mills along the banks. This is in fact the source of the town's present name, for Torre Molino means Tower of the Mills.

Shortly after the fall of Granada in the 15th century, Torremolinos was frequently subject to pirate attacks and other offenses from the sea, with the population plummeting to a mere 106 inhabitants in 1769. Largely rebuilt in the first half of the 19th century, the milling industry once again became Torremolinos' main driving force, only to meet its slow decline less than a century later.

In the early 20th century, Torremolinos was a mostly fishing- and agriculture-devoted town of 3,000 residents. Nowadays, over a quarter of a million people fill up its beaches and streets during the summer, temporarily bringing up its population above levels common for much bigger cities across Spain.

This can all be traced back to the late 1950s, when a major tourist boom hit the small town and Torremolinos embarked on a journey of development, quickly becoming the top tourist destination in all of Andalusia. Torremolinos is the home of the first luxury hotel opened on the coast (Pez Espada in 1959) as well as the first gay bar (Toni's Bar in 1962) and has always been a step ahead of its coastal neighbors. The de-facto birthplace of tourism in all of Costa del Sol, its history is tightly packed with celebrity names as well; popular icons such as Ernest Hemingway, Brigitte Bardot and Frank Sinatra have walked its streets and worshipped its beaches.

Crowds still throng the beaches of Torremolinos in the summer. Hotels, apartment buildings, restaurants, bars and clubs all provide a backdrop to the dark-sanded long stretches. However, should you wish to escape the sun lounger and the tourist developments, head to the outskirts of the town where forests and springs will provide a much-needed change of scenery. If you would rather explore urban Torremolinos and its definite touch of traditional, head to the historic Calle San Miguel in the center or check out the old fishing cottages in La Carihuela.

If you think Torremolinos is adventure-packed during the day, wait until the sun comes down. Easily one of the loudest party capitals in the Costa del Sol, the town caters to a wide range of tastes when it comes to nightlife – from high-end dining to free-flowing sangria in the numerous bars and clubs in the brash La Nogalera, Torremolinos is sure to intrigue every taste. And if you are looking for something extra, check out neighboring Benalmadena with its award-winning marina and theme parks or nearby province-capital Malaga, both of which provide at least a day of sightseeing-packed agenda.

Culture

Despite being a town inhabited for over 150,000 years, Torremolinos' main selling point has always been its beachfront. Letting loose seems to be the theme as tourists from all over the world bask in the sun, sip cocktails and party until dawn. But flicking through a history book unveils a story of mixed cultures, with Romans, Greeks, Phoenicians, Moors and Arabs all intertwined in a complex amalgam of influences.

Head to the end of San Miguel Street for a whiff of Moorish architecture as you climb the 14th century Pimentel Tower or check out the San Miguel church dedicated to the town's patron saint. For spectacular neo-Mudejar architecture, stroll by the Navajas' House of Knives. If this does not seem enough, then do give nearby Malaga a try, with its historic Alcazaba, a Renaissance Cathedral and – above all – a rich Picasso heritage.

Do not forget to indulge your taste buds as well, for Torremolinos is Spain's seafood capital. If you have a chance, participate in the annual Fried Fish Day (Dia del Pescaito), taking place on the first Thursday in June on La Carihuela Beach. Other annual events worth planning your trip around are the Festival of the Virgin in La Carihuela (July 16) and the San Miguel Festival (September 29) with celebrations and festivities organized all over town.

Location & Orientation

Only 13 kilometers southwest of Malaga and served by the A-7 motorway, Torremolinos could not be easier to access. A regular train service connects it to both the city of Malaga and its airport (about 30 minutes ride) as well as provides easy access to coastal points further south, all the way down to Fuengirola.

If you are visiting Torremolinos with your own vehicle during the high season, be ready for parking difficulties anywhere in the city center. A regular local bus service covers most of the town (cost €1.25 per ride); though walking through Torremolinos can be quite charming, particularly along its beachfront promenade.

A magnificent rock formation splits Torremolinos' into two sections: the beach of El Bajondillo to the left extends into the adjoining beaches of Playamar and Los Alamos Look to the right you will see the Castillo de Santa Clara, with the La Carihuela and Montemar beaches just near it. These two parts used to be cut off from each other until the promenade Paseo Maritimo was extended around the rock and now continues all the way to lovely Benalmadena's marina, a mere 30-minute walk away.

Climate & When to Visit

Even though summer is by far the most popular time to visit Torremolinos, the town has positioned itself as a year-round destination unlike other cities along the Costa del Sol. Winters are mild here, with temperatures almost never falling below 10°C (50°F) and could be a good time to visit for those wanting to avoid the summer crowds.

June and September are an excellent time to visit Torremolinos as well, with plenty of sun, average temperatures around 26°C (79°F) and more affordable prices. But if you want to see Torremolinos during peak-season, be prepared for both higher price tags and temperatures as well, with averages around 29°C (82°F) and highs sometimes reaching 38°C (100°F).

Money & Currency

The official currency in all of Spain is the Euro. Prices and costs of a vacation in Torremolinos can be highly variable depending on your choice of accommodation and entertainment. However, as a general rule and compared to some of the other coastal cities in Spain, Torremolinos can be quite affordable. If you come to party, set aside a considerable amount of your budget for cocktails. As anywhere in Europe, seek out fixed-price menus and take advantage of the many excellent seafood restaurants with competitive tapas' prices.

Sightseeing Highlights

Paseo Maritimo

Torremolinos' seafront promenade Paseo Maritimo stretches for 7 kilometers and is a prime example of a well-cared-for beach walkway. Starting from the Playamar and ending at Benalmadena's port, the promenade is clad with benches, palm trees and over 200 beach bars and restaurants. Look out for some of the interesting sculptures that have also found there home here and admire the gorgeous sea views and the interesting rock formations of the area.

El Bajondillo Beach

The 1.1-kilometer-long and 40-meter-wide beach of El Bajondillo - to the east of the cliff that separates Torremolinos into two - is an urban beach with dark sand, lined with numerous eateries and hotels. Sunbeds, toilets and showers are all available on the beach and there is a general sense of ongoing maintenance. But the biggest selling point for El Bajondillo must be the chiringuitos that run along the beach and provide a welcome variation in styles and décor. Families with children will be pleasantly surprised with the play area for the youngest beach-lovers. Sports facilities such as beach volleyball also add to the appeal of this locals-favorite beach that is particularly packed during July and August.

La Carihuela

Emblematically Spanish, the neighborhood of La Carihuela still features fishermen cottages and is the national mecca for seafood-lovers. Just west of Torremolinos' center, this quarter was traditionally a fishing village and though time has taken its toll on its fishing identity, reminders of a sea-centered life are everywhere. Bougainvillea-dressed terraces, classical small houses and excellent seafood restaurants seem to define the picturesque area where the cosmopolitan meets the traditional with the pleasant aroma of fried pescaito fish permanently lingering in the air.

Andalucian Torremolinos' culinary fame is longstanding and well-earned specifically because of La Carihuela's pescaito frito; the small fried fish popular everywhere in Spain seem to taste much better here than anywhere else in the country. But beyond fish, La Carihuela has always held the key to Torremolinos' popularity as it was the select travel destination of celebrities and high society figures starting from the 1950s, thus propelling the small town into worldwide fame.

The pedestrian boardwalk invites a leisurely stroll and is the favorite gathering place for local families and tourists alike, with many restaurants, chiringuitos and hotels. Next to it is the La Carihuela beach – a 2.1 kilometers long stretch perfect for families and trend-setters alike. You can lounge lazily on a beach bed in the shade of a palm tree or you can opt for an hour of jet skiing or pedal boating; either way, La Carihuela easily pleases all guests. This vast Blue Flag beach was actually the first Costa del Sol beach to receive international tourists in the mid-20th century, with jet setters such as Frank Sinatra and Sophia Loren vacationing here during its early fame days.

If you visit Torremolinos in the peak of the summer, you may want to plan your visit around July 16, when La Carihuela celebrates its Virgen del Carmen patron saint as sailors carry the Virgin's throne into the sea, requesting her blessing.

Calle San Miguel

Away from the beachfront and undoubtedly the heart of Torremolinos, pedestrian Calle San Miguel exudes the cosmopolitan atmosphere so typical of this small coastal city. The street is a great case study of the entrepreneurial spirit surviving in a constantly globalizing tourism industry, with tantalizing small craft shops and street entertainers competing for the visitors' attention.

Head here for a solid dose of people-watching and delightful ice cream sold by street vendors or a leisurely glass of sangria; the ambiance is genuinely cozy, traditional and typical and is a natural magnet for tourists. Torremolinos has managed to preserve this real treasure of a pedestrian street, with much if it remaining relatively unchanged in the past decades. Here, you can find original tobacco shops, stationery shops, jewelry sellers and a well-stocked liquor store where some of the spirits are over 30 years old.

Calle San Miguel ends at Custa del Tajo, where steep steps (or an elevator) lead you down to El Bajondillo.

Church of San Miguel

Plaza de San Miguel, 29620 Torremolinos
Tel: +34 952 380 805
http://www.diocesismalaga.es/index.php?mod=parros
&secc=detall&cod=2212

One of the most authentic historical buildings in
Torremolinos, the Church of Saint Michael on Calle San
Miguel is dedicated to the patron saint of the city.
Housing a number of artifacts from various periods
inside, this whitewashed church with two bell towers also
features an iron figure of the saint. The interior is
modestly decorated but does include interesting ceiling
carvings, an ornate altar and stained glass windows. The
atmosphere inside the church is quiet and can truly be a
welcome break from the busy streets nearby. Entrance is
free.

For a full week in late September of each year, festivities
in honor of San Miguel take place in Torremolinos and
the procession always starts in this small parish church.
The procession carries the statue of San Miguel perched
on a heavy chest decorated with flowers and moves to the
accompanying beat of a drum, truly one of the most
popular religious festivities in all of Spain.

Pimentel Tower

At the foot of Calle San Miguel towards the beach, the 12-meter-high Torre de Pimentel greets you and unfolds its long history. Previously known as Torre de los Molinos, Torre de Molinos or even Torre Molinos (all meaning "tower of the mills"), the tower is a landmark that has granted its name to the city and is a major historic point of interest in Torremolinos. Dating back to 1300 when Spain was under Moorish rule, the tower was built from adobe and earth in order to protect invasions by North African pirates coming in from the sea. Constructed by Nasrid rulers from Granada, it was also used as a mill. Later on, the tower was renamed in honor of Don Rodrigo de Pimentel, a notable figure who greatly donated to the Catholic Kings during their Malaga and Granada conquests.

Entrance to the tower is free and it is open daily. Head to the top floor of the tower for spectacular panoramic city and beach views.

House of Knives (Casa de los Navajas)

Calle Las Mercedes, 29620 Torremolinos

Property of the Municipality of Torremolinos, the historic landmark building known as Casa de los Navajas is a small residential palace built in 1925 for Antonio Navajas, a well-known entrepreneur in the sugar cane business.

The heirs of Antonio Navajas loaned the property to the city, which closed it down in 2000 for an extensive renovation. This is truly one of Torremolinos' best-known buildings and the city has planned to spend at least half a million euros on its revitalization.

Set on a cliff overlooking El Bajondillo, the two-floor building was constructed in a neo-mudejar style, very typical in the province of Malaga in the late 19th and early 20th centuries. The first floor comprises four bedrooms, bathrooms, a living room and a kitchen while a large living area and two round towers can be found on the second floor. The interior decorations are inspired by the Alhambra in Granada while the tile work on the exterior was sourced from the Toledo and Talavera tile factories.

Because of its ongoing renovation status, the house is not open to the public but you can nevertheless marvel at its exterior's beautiful architecture and particularly interesting location. Look for the house in the Torremolinos nighttime skyline as it is illuminated, providing a majestic sight.

Nightlife & Clubbing

Torremolinos is sure to please most when the sun sets down: whether a night out means a dinner and a stroll along the beach or dancing in a club until dawn, you can be certain that you will not be disappointed here. This is a cosmopolitan place where nightlife takes many shapes and forms, with most of the clubs located on the main San Miguel street or in the La Nogalera area.

For the younger crowds, there are quite a few places, including the three-floor Paladium (particularly popular with teenagers), Fun Beach on Calle Mallorca, Kiss Bar on the central Plaza next to Calle San Miquel, Tinas Bar at the top of Calle San Miquel and the truly loud techno-heaven Voltage.

If you are on the hunt for a truly unusual club, visit Pipers – a frequent venue for live acts, featuring a plane suspended from the ceiling.

The sometimes-rowdy Plaza Nogalera has quite a few options up its sleeve as well. If you are a Karaoke fan, check out El Open Arms. Pool players should head to Bel Air while beer enthusiasts should try La Cervezateca, just opposite the Pueblo Blanco. Rock music seeps out of Garfields, also in La Nogalera.

In La Carihuela, check out Atrevete where salsa dancing and a true party atmosphere are sure to keep you entertained until dawn.

Torremolinos also has a thriving LGBT community and is a gay friendly destination. One of the trendiest gay bars in the city is El Gato Lounge on Paseo Maritimo. Excellent tapas, cocktails and wine have consistently made El Gato one of Costa del Sol's most famous bars.

Battery Park (Parque la Bateria)

If you are visiting Torremolinos with children, do not skip the 74,000 square meter Parque la Bateria – a hidden gem that is free to enter as well. Opened to the public in 2007, this park is a little off the beaten track and used to house military barracks until the 1950s. Inside it, among other things, is a 15-meter-high tower with a spiral staircase. Make it a point to climb up (or take the elevator), as the views over Malaga from the top are truly stunning.

A rather large adventure area for children is sure to keep young ones entertained while grownups will find true relaxations in the gorgeously landscaped gardens and under the shades of many types of trees, with the sound of chirping birds as a permanent soundtrack. A large artificial lake with a Baroque fountain completes the idyllic park picture, with boats available for rent for €1 per hour.

Head to the "dummy tree" if you are traveling with toddlers who are working on giving up their dummies – this is a place to let go of this childhood accessory in a truly unusual manner. Parents and young ones place dummies in plastic balls, sign and date them, and leave them hanging from this unusual tree.

To get to the Battery Park, head west from the center of Torremolinos (using the old N340 going around the center). Free parking is available. The park is open daily from 11:00 to midnight in the summertime, from 11:00 to 21:00 in the spring and fall and from 11:00 to 20:00 in the winter months. The park opens later on Mondays (from 17:30). No pets are allowed in the park.

Botanic Garden Molina de Inca

Nueva Ronda de Circunvalacion Oeste, 29620 Torremolinos

In the northern area of Torremolinos, the Molina de Inca is a lovely way to spend a few hours in one of Spain's most famous botanic gardens. At the turn of the 18th century, the city of Malaga allowed Joseph de Inca Sotomayor to build two mills on what is today the garden's location. The mills produced some of the finest flour nation-wide with the use of a mountain spring that propelled them. Today, the mills are still operational and are the focal point in the gardens that otherwise feature over 500 varieties of trees, including over 70 types of palm trees.

Some of the most interesting species of trees found in the garden include the tall century-old Araucaria, as well as Eucaliptus and Ficus, among others. A circular maze and 12 bird-inhabited aviaries are also some of the garden's most interesting features. Owls, falcons, macaws and other exotic birds have found home here among ponds, fountains and marble statues.

Entrance to the botanic garden costs €3 and the garden is open Tuesday to Sunday from 11:30 to 14:00 and 18:00 to 21:00 in the summertime and from 10:30 to 14:00 and 16:00 to 18:00 in the winter.

Aqualand

C/Cuba 10, Torremolinos
Tel: +34 952 38 88 88
http://www.aqualand.es/torremolinos/en/

You can easily spend a whole day in Costa del Sol's largest waterpark just near Torremolinos. Waterslides, water rides and a water playground for children are only some of the activities offered in Aqualand. No less than 30 different slides (for both adults and children) are available, with some of the most popular being the 100-meter-drop Black Hole, the rafting-like rapids' rides and the dizzying Boomerang – a float ride on a slippery surface. For those that are more inclined to relaxation rather than an adrenaline rush, the Tropical Lagoon is a perfect place to relax, as is the Jacuzzi pool.

The Aqualand is near the Botanical Garden and can either be accessed by taxi from Torremolinos' center or – if traveling with a car – via the motorway exit at Palace of Congress. Unlike other similar parks, Aqualand allows visitors to bring their own food, so you do not have to rely on the overpriced park eateries.

Tickets for the Aqualand are best purchased online, though visitors should be aware that they are only valid from the day after they are purchased. Admission costs €23.40 for adults, €16.65 for children 5-10 years old and €10 for those under four.

Crocodile Park

Calle Cuba, 14, Torremolinos
Tel: +34 952 051 78
http://www.cocodrilospark.com/index.html

This crocodile-specialized park is the home to over 300 crocodiles that live in its eight lakes. A nursery for baby crocodiles, an African style fortress, a children playground as well as a souvenir shop are all included in the park's grounds.

The most interesting aspect of the park is the crocodile exhibition, taking place several times a day, during which Europe's largest crocodile weighing 600kg – called Big Daddy – is shown to the audience. As a stark contrast, visitors can also take photos with a baby crocodile.

Two-hour tours are available and the guides are very knowledgeable and entertaining. The ticket costs €15.50 for adults, €13.00 for children 4-12. Admission is free for children under four. The Crocodile Park is open from 10:00 to 19:00 during summertime, 10:00 to 18:00 in March, April, May and October and 10:00 to 17:00 in the winter months.

Benalmadena

Located in the heart of Costa del Sol, Benalmadena is Torremolinos' neighbor and certainly has enough to offer for a whole day (or two) of sightseeing and adventure. Only 6 kilometers from the center of Torremolinos, it is easily accessible by car, train, bus or even by foot along the coastal promenade.

Nowadays made up of three distinct town sections (Benalmadena Pueblo, Arroyo de la Miel and coastal Benalmadena) it has a long history dating to prehistoric times, with a spectacular development evident during the Muslim rule period. It is today one of the main destinations for tourists visiting the Costa del Sol and features many adventure-related attractions and a lovely marina.

Benalmadena Old Town (Pueblo)

Located in the upper part of the city, Benalmadena Pueblo is a whitewashed town with narrow cobblestone streets, jasmine trees and a gorgeous town square. Sitting on top of a hill some 300 meters above sea level, the old town used to be occupied by Romans and Moors and the architecture certainly reflects this heritage. Views from the old town over the Costa del Sol are truly unparalleled.

Puerto Marina

Benalmadena's port is an award-winning marina, having won the "Best Marina in the World" title more than once. With 1,100 boat moorings, a cutting-edge architecture and artificial islands, it is the most cosmopolitan area of Benalmadena. Dozens of shops, restaurants, bars and clubs provide additional interest both during the daytime as well as at night.

There are numerable activities you can participate in at the Marina - from hiring a boat or lounging by the Blue Flag beach through a wide range of watersports and all the way to fine dining, the marina seems to be a thriving social point not only for Benalmadena but also for the wider coastal area.

For a particularly interesting way to experience the marina, hop on the restored Mississippi Willow steamer boat and enjoy a late afternoon cruise.

Sea Life

Puerto Marina, s/n, Benalmádena
Tel: +34 952 56 01 50
http://www.visitsealife.com/benalmadena/en/

Children and adults alike will find themselves truly immersed in sea's wonders in the fascinating Sea Life, popular all over Costa del Sol. Here at this walk-through underwater park you can see and even touch creatures like sea cucumbers, sea urchins, starfish and crabs. Sea species from virtually all oceans of the world swim by you as you explore the park and its 30 tanks with reproduced natural habitats.

Feeding demonstrations, nurseries and other theme-focused presentations are also some of the additional features of Sea Life. The park is located at the Benalmadena marina and is open daily from 10:00 to midnight. Adult admission costs €16.25 (€11.25 if purchased online); € 14.00 (€ 9.00 for online purchase) for children under 11.

Tivoli World

Arroyo de la Miel, Benalmádena
Tel: +34 952 57 70 16
http://www.tivoli.es/

Costa del Sol's largest and most popular amusement park provides a wide range of entertainment options for the whole family, including musical performances, adventure rides and various shows. A number of squares are found throughout the park, all focused on a specific theme, such as Western, Jungle or Andalusia. Magician shows, mini disco, flamenco performances and over 30 different rides can be enjoyed, ranging from merry-go-rounds to adrenaline-inducing water slides.

Unlike similar amusement parks, Tivoli World is open daily from 18:00 to 02:00 in the summer time due to the hot weather. During the rest of the year the opening hours are subject to various schedules and changes, so check the park's website for more accurate information.

Entrance into the park costs € 7.95 for anyone that is over 1 meter tall, free otherwise. Rides and other attractions are subject to additional costs and visitors have the option to either purchase a Supertivolino ticket (€ 13.95) which includes admission to all the rides or separate Tivolinos (mostly costing € 2) for each ride.

You can take exit number 222 from the A7 highway to get to Tivoli World, or take a taxi to get there from Benalmadena's center. Alternatively, you can also take the bus; stop Tivoli in Arroyo de la Miel.

Malaga

This province's capital is sure to delight with its historic architecture, artistic heritage and exciting shopping opportunities. Swap the Torremolinos' beaches for a day of exploring and you will not regret it.

Cathedral

Calle Molina Lario, 9, Malaga
Tel.:+34 952220345
http://www.diocesismalaga.es/index.php?mod=catedral

The Renaissance Malaga Cathedral known as La Manquita was constructed between 1528 and 1782 for the Catholic Monarch. Built on a rectangular plan drawn by Diego de Siloe, it includes 17th-century choir stalls by Pedro de Mena. Unlike the interior, the façade is a pure Baroque work with portals, marble columns and stone-carved medallions of the patron saints. The sanctuary is filled with artworks, including a Gothic as well as a neoclassical altarpiece in addition to the 16th-century tombs and sculptures by Palomino and Salazar

The 84-meter tower adds height to the Malaga Cathedral, making it the second highest one in all of Andalusia. The Cathedral is located in the historic center of Malaga, on a site that was previously occupied by Moors.

Alcazaba

c/Alcazabilla, s/n, Malaga
Tel: +34 952 22 72 30

Malaga's magnificent Alcazaba, built by the Mannudid dynasty in the 11th century, is Spain's best-preserved Moorish fortress palace. It is often considered as a prototype of Taifa period military architecture and has two walled enclosures. Perched on a hill in the center of Malaga, the Alcazaba features an outer citadel entrance as well as elevator access. Gardens with elaborate decorations, magnificent gateways and towers are all part of the magic fortress, as is the internal citadel's palace including the living quarters of kings and governors.

After the Reconquista, the Alcazaba fell into decay only to be rediscovered in 1933 when slow restorations commenced and are still ongoing. The fortress is connected to the nearby castle Castillo Gibralfaro though a passageway.

Head here for a heavy dose of Moorish architecture but also for spectacular views over Malaga and its port. Entrance into the Alcazaba costs €2.10 (€3.45 if combined with a visit to Castillo Gibralfaro). Free tours are available from 14:00 until closing time on Sundays. The Alcazaba is open from 09:30 to 20:00 in the summer, 08:30 to 19:00 in the wintertime.

Calle Larios

Also known as Marques de Larios, this 19th century street in has been Malaga's landmark since 1891. Currently it is the fifth most expensive shopping street in all of Spain and among the 50 most expensive in all of Europe. Come here to check out the monument to Manuel Domingo Larios y Larios - the firstborn son of Marques de Larios - responsible for the street's construction.

The architecture of the street is of major interest as well. All of the 12 blocks of buildings feature four floors and standardized attics, curved corners, French windows and wrought iron railings. Pastel colors give the street a characteristic charm while the marble sidewalks additionally augment it.

Make sure you visit the street in the late afternoon and early evening, when locals promenade and enjoy a drink and a round of tapas. Shopaholics are also sure to love Calle Larios, due to its numerous clothing and shoe shops.

Picasso Museum

Palacio de Buenavista, c/San Agustín, 8, Malaga
Tel: +34 902 44 33 77
http://www.museopicassomalaga.org/

Pablo Ruiz Picasso was born in Malaga and the city is still very much proud of this fact. Over 280 works of the artist are currently on display in the Museo Picasso Malaga, opened since 2003.

The Museum is located only 200 meters from Picasso's birthplace on Plaza de la Merced.

Housed in the Buenavista Palace dating from the early 16th century and itself a National Monument, the Museum sprawls into 18 more houses from the old Jewish quarters and occupies a total area of 8,300 square meters. Some of the most famous pieces on display at the Museum include "Olga Kokhlova with Mantila", "Portrait of Paulo with White Hat" and "Mother and Child". The Museum is within a short walking distance of the Cathedral.

The museum is open daily except Mondays, from 10:00 to 20:00 (21:00 on Fridays and Saturdays). Admission to the permanent collection costs € 6; temporary exhibitions € 4.50. A combined visit costs € 9 whereas entrance is free from 15:00 onwards on every last Sunday of the month.

Recommendations for the Budget Traveller

Places To Stay

Hotel Mediterraneo Carihuela

C/Carmen 43, 29620 Torremolinos
Tel: +34 952 381 452
http://mediterraneohotel.es/

The 3-star Mediterraneo in front of La Carihuela beach is an attractive and affordable solution for those looking for beachfront accommodation in Torremolinos. The hotel's 36 rooms are all traditionally decorated, with balconies, TV, fridge and kitchenette in some. The hotel optionally organizes shuttle transportation from the Malaga Airport. A number of traditional Spanish restaurants can be found near the hotel.

Twin rooms at the Mediterraneo Carihuela start at €30 per night during September, €50 during May and €60 in the highest season. Optional breakfast costs € 5 per person per night.

Villa Albero

Av de Carlota Alessandri 82, 29620 Torremolinos
Tel: +34 952 388 373
http://www.villa-albero.com/

This 15-room family-owned hotel near the La Carihuela beach was built in 1968. Refurbished recently, the atmosphere at the Albero is cozy and perfectly complements the ideal location just steps from the beach. The hotel has a lovely enclosed courtyard as well as rooms featuring A/C and satellite TV. Albero is located right next to a bus stop and has a wide range of shops, bars and restaurants within walking distance.

Prices at the Albero vary depending on your room of choice and time of visit and start from €30 per night for a twin room in the early fall season (September) but can easily triple during the summer months.

Hotel Natursun

Avenida Carlota Alessandri 1,
corner of Pasaje Santa Mónica,
29620 Torremolinos
Tel: +34 951 241 364
http://www.hotelnatursun.com/

Hotel Natursun is yet another very conveniently located accommodation option for those wanting to be close to the lovely Carihuela beach as it is within walking distance of this Blue Flag stretch. This modern hotel provides bright and airy rooms with minimalist décor, flat-screen TV, free Wi-Fi and private terraces. An outdoor pool can also be found on the premises as well as a restaurant serving Mediterranean cuisine.

Rates for a double room in this value hotel start at €48 per night (breakfast included) in May or September, but can quickly double during the highest season (July and August).

Hostal Guadalupe

Del Peligro 15, 29620 Torremolinos
Tel: +34 952 381 937
http://www.hostalguadalupe.com/

If you would rather be closer to Torremolinos' center, check out Hostal Guadalupe – a bed and breakfast with 18 rooms.

With all rooms tastefully decorated and with private terraces or balconies, the hostal is located only 100 meters away from the popular El Bajondillo beach in the center of the city. The friendly staff completes the welcoming atmosphere in the traditionally Spanish Guadalupe that provides excellent value for money.

Standard double of twin rooms at Hostal Guadalupe start at about €55 per night in the low season, including breakfast. Unlike some of the other establishments in Torremolinos, the hostal does not exhibit extreme variations between seasons, with typical high season prices usually only slightly higher.

Hotel Casa Rosa

Pensamiento 31, 29639 Benalmádena
Tel: +34 952 568 047
http://www.hotelcasarosabenalmadena.com/

If Benalmadena has enchanted you with its marina and adventure-packed agenda, consider spending a night in one of its many hotels. Hotel Casa Rosa is an affordable one-star hotel right in the center of the town, its bright rooms with terraces offering sea views. Some of the other amenities include free Wi-Fi, safe, minibar and plasma TV. The beaches of Benalmadena are 2.5 kilometers away.

Prices for one of the 14 standard twin rooms at the lovely Casa Rosa start at around €50 per night year-round. Breakfast costs additional € 5.90 per person per night.

Places To Eat & Drink

El Sabor

Calle Casablanca 20, 29620 Torremolinos
Tel: +34 952 384 069
http://www.elsabor.net/

This award-winning international cuisine restaurant with
a decidedly Scandinavian twist is a short walk from
Torremolinos' center. The interior is refined with a
relaxed ambiance and the food is excellent with generous
servings. Try the superb salmon tartar or reindeer tartar
(€7), the stuffed chicken fillet (€13.50) or the king prawns
in garlic and chili oil (€8.20) before sampling some of El
Sabor's desserts (starting from €4.80). Wines start at about
€ 10 per bottle.

El Gato Lounge

Paseo Maritimo de 1, 29620 Torremolinos
Tel: +34 687 871 165

In addition to being one of Torremolinos' iconic venues,
El Gato Lounge offers excellent reasonably-priced food
and exquisite wines served by attentive staff. Located on
the beachfront, the lounge also provides guests with the
option to enjoy their food and drink at the beach chairs
right at the sand.

Many tapas options are on the menu, including a set price 'Tapas Box' (€25) with a dozen of various items, as well as a wide range of salads (from €5.90), large bruschettas (from €4.90) and burgers (from €5.50). Over 50 types of cocktails are also served at the famous El Gato.

Granvinos

Calle Santos Arcangeles 4,
Corner of Plaza San Miguel 5,
29620 Torremolinos
Tel: +34 952 058 939

This distinctly Spanish restaurant serves authentic national food and provides a very courteous service in a setting slightly off the typical tourist route. Order one of the starter platters (sufficient to feed two people) and then try the Basque-inspired cod in garlic sauce, or the lamb chops. Expect to pay around €50 for a very filling dinner for two, with excellent house wine. Note that the restaurant is closed on Tuesdays.

Matahambre

Calle de las Mercedes 14, 29620 Torremolinos
Tel: +34 95 238 1242
http://matahambre.com/

Essentially a bodega selling wines and spirits, Matahambre offers interesting tapas and is a locals' favorite in Torremolinos.

Try the unusual combinations such as cheese with fruit jelly, salmon and honey or the air-dried tuna. Prices for tapas start from €3. Matahambre also serves an excellent Ribera del Duero house wine. For dessert, try the delicious hot brownie with ice cream.

El Meson de Cervantes

Calle Alamos, 11, 29012, 29012 Malaga
Tel: +34 952 2162 74
http://www.elmesondecervantes.com

Take a break from sightseeing and art in Malaga and check out the wildly popular El Meson de Cervantes, a favorite tapas bar for tourists and locals alike. With fresh ingredients and creative combinations, the restaurant has two sections: a more formal sit-down dinner hall as well as a relaxed tapas bar in the front.

Some of the most creative tapas include the smoked salmon stuffed with Russian Salad, the Iberian pork with pumpkin and pineapple and the lamb sweetbreads with chimichurri. Each dish comes in tapa-size serving (prices from €2.50 to €4), half portion or full portion serving (from €7.50 to €14). Excellent wines start from €12 per bottle. Unless you are truly full, give the fig flan a try – spiked with sweet Malaga wine, it is a true delight.

Places To Shop

Cortefiel Torremolinos

Av.Palma De Mallorca 5, 29620 Torremolinos
Tel: +34 952 370 212
http://cortefiel.com/

Check out the popular Cortefiel department store, part of
the Cortefiel chain present in over 20 countries with more
than 350 stores. Trendy fashion at affordable prices and
frequent sales and reductions (particularly during the
summer) are sure to delight avid shoppers, with clothing
lines mostly targeted to the 35-45 age group.

Les Tres Torres

Calle San Miguel 17, 29620 Torremolinos

If you are hunting for unique souvenirs, particularly
those targeted to art-lovers, check out Les Tres Torres on
the central Calle San Miguel, which stocks a wide variety
of refined and stylish items. Some of the products sold
here include Toledo-steel souvenirs, Seville-sourced
ceramics as well as Majorica pearls.

Montinas

La Nogalera 26, 29620 Torremolinos
Tel: +34 952 381 178
http://www.montinas.com/

Montinas gift shop, located in the La Nogalera area, is a traditional and quaint store with a very large selection of gifts and souvenirs, well known all over Spain. Traditional souvenirs such as castanets compete with modern trinkets such as Swarovsky crystals and Majorica jewelry. If you find yourself craving too many gifts to carry back home, the store will conveniently ship them to you at tax-free factory prices.

Arroyo De La Miel Flea Market

Benalmadena

On Fridays, head to the Arroyo de la Miel flea market in Benalmadena, where a wide range of goods and their haggle-ready sellers await you. This large flea markets sells anything from leather goods to fruits and vegetables including home ware, clothing, souvenirs and pottery.

Atarazanas Central Market

Calles de las Atarazanas, Malaga

Hungry tourists and foodies alike will definitely find their paradise in the Atarazanas Central Market in Malaga. What is likely to start as a food-souvenir shopping trip is surely to develop into an unforgettable culinary experience, as the fresh seafood, breads and produce seem to beckon from every stall. Hunt for the aceitunas alinadas (local olives) and the fried salted almonds or look for high-quality saffron as well as other spices.

Fuengirola & Benalmadena

Fuengirola and Benalmadena are popular tourist destinations on the Spanish Costa del Sol in Andalusia and the towns overlook the beautiful azure waters of the Mediterranean. The area attracts Europeans who want a holiday in the sun.

The area is full of beaches, bars and restaurants (many under expatriate British ownership) but you will also find more typically Spanish influences including flamenco, bullfighting, and Moorish-influenced architecture.

The province of Malaga is located in Spain's famed Costa del Sol region and you will probably fly into Malaga. Malaga is Europe's southernmost major city and one of the oldest cities of the world. It is also where the internationally renowned painter and sculptor Pablo Picasso was born, as well as the actor Antonio Banderas.

http://www.fuengirola.es/portal_localweb/InitIndex.do
http://www.andalucia.com/benalmadena/home.htm

Culture

The sun-drenched touristic towns of Fuengirola and Benalmadena have many cultural attractions. In October, there is a colorful fiesta that is held every year in honor of the Virgen del Rosario. There is also the fiesta of the Virgen del Carmen (patron saint of the sea) which is held in July. There are celebrations for Holy Week which starts in April and the night of San Juan Sheikh takes place at the summer solstice. In August the Festival Cuidad de Fuengirola takes place in the castle.

As you walk through the alleys and lanes of these towns, you will see their Arab and Moorish influences, especially in the architecture. That is easily seen in the Arab Baths, watch towers, and castles which give these towns an exotic flare. You can also see the Roman influence when you visit the Roman pillars and sculptures which date back to 2nd century B.C.

From Fuengirola harbor, you can take a ride on Aqua Vista which is a glass-bottomed boat where you can view the beauty of what lies under the sea without getting wet. If you are a scuba diver and love experiencing underwater treasures first hand, there is the Fuengirola Diving Center where there are diving expedition and classes available.

There are also mini-cruises that usually run all twelve months of the year. If fishing is your thing, then this harbor is also for you. It offers fishing trips that run daily with meals on board. There is also tuna fishing. There is also parasailing at this harbor called Smile High Parasailing which you can do alone or in a group of no less than five people.

Fuengirola has a prominent zoo, several open parks, and historical sites like the famous sea-front Suhail Castle which was renovated in 2000 and began hosting festivals and summer concerts shortly after. The Castle dates back to the 17th century. There is the Plaza de la Constitucion (Old Church Square) which is located at the center of the town, the Plaza de Toros (bullring) and the Fuengirola museum. You'll be happy to know that there is also a large Aquapark on the outskirts of Fuengirola which is open from April to September to help you cool off during those hot summer months.

You could also take a 20-minute bus ride to the village of Mijas where you can enjoy this picturesque village as you take a stroll through its streets and through the hills of the Sierras as you look out onto the Mediterranean and Fuengirola below. And if you enjoy dancing the night away, there is a wide variety of late night entertainment on the Fuengirola seafront where most of the action takes place.

Location & Orientation

Fuengirola is a large town and municipality of *Costa del Sol*. it is a major tourist resort and has more than 8km of beaches with a winding promenade called *Paseo Maritimo*, which is the longest promenade in Spain. Palm trees line the walkway as well as the benches, flowers, shops, restaurants, bars, and year-round great weather.

The beaches are holders of the Blue Flag award which is given to beaches based on their high standards for water quality, safety, environmental management. There are 17 beaches which are all Blue Flag holders. They are all well equipped especially the beaches on the eastern side of Benalmadena. The ones on the western front, however, are rocky so they are better equipped for fishing or diving. Be advised that one of the beaches on the west end, Benalnatura, is a nudist beach.

This charming town is nestled between Benalmadena in the northeast and Mijas to the north. It is located about 15 minutes west of Malaga airport. Fuengirola lies at the foothills of the Sierra de Mijas which can be seen from the Fuengirola Harbor.

Benalmadena is located 15km south west of Malaga. It is known for its dynamic nighttime entertainment, excellent cuisine, and sunny beaches. The town is divided into three main urban centers: Benalmadena Costa where all the magnificent beaches are, Benalmadena Pueblo, a picturesque village with great views overlooking the Mediterranean, and Arroyo de la Miel (Honey Brook) which is the economic center and where you will find the train station. The name of Benalmadena comes from the Arabic "Ibn-al-Madena" which means "son of the mines" due to the presence of several iron mines in the vicinity.

If you like to party, then Benalmadena and Fuengirola is for you. Enjoying the breezy nights and dancing under the stars is what this area is famous for. When the sun sets (and before) the pubs and discos come alive. Head out to one of the most highlighted centers on the Costa de Sol, *Puerto Marina* in Benalmadena and party all night long. The discos and pubs there usually open around 11pm. The downside is that these places can be a bit pricey. Benalmadena Marina has been recognized as 'the best marina in the world' twice since 1987.

Among the interesting things you'll find in Benalmadena is a monument that is located in front of the Plaza del Remo on the promenade. This monument is dedicated to fishermen working in the area's fishing industry. And among the interesting places you can visit are a real ice-skating rink located on Avenida Garcia Lorca, the Tivoli World Theme Park which among its many rides and attractions holds a weekly Friday morning street market in the car park, Selwo Marina with its cute penguins and dolphins and the Sealife Center which houses a walk-through Lost City of Atlantis where you could see marine life swimming all around you.

You could also take a ride in the Teleferico (Cable Car) which will take you 769m up the Monte Calamarro where you will get a chance to look out at the coastline below, and on a clear day, you could even see the coast of North Africa in the distance. It's an eight minute ride.

There is a modern train system that connects Fuengirola and Benalmadena to Malaga Airport with other stops along the way. These trains are equipped with TV screens that highlight the name of the up-coming stop and how long it will take to get there. The names are announced in Spanish and English. The train runs from 5:30am from the Malaga Centro-Alameda train station and runs until 10:30pm. You can purchase tickets at each station via an interactive touch-screen from which you can select your language of choice. Take good care of your ticket because you will need it to enter and exit the turnstiles at the train platform.

Climate & When to Visit

http://www.eltiempo24.es/

Benalmadena has an elevation of 800m above sea-level. The area gets up to 15 hours of daylight in June with temperatures reaching 26°C (78.8°F), sometimes as high as 30°C (86°F) in August when the humidity spikes. The minimum nighttime temperature is typically 19°C (66.2°F) in July and August.

Temperatures in the winter months reach as low as 15°C (59°F) with night time temperatures going as low as 7°C (44.6°F). Rainfall levels are at their highest during the months of October through March. The temperature of the sea water ranges from its highest of 23°C (73.4°F) in August to its lowest of 15°C (59°F) in February and March.

The best time to visit Fuengirola and Benalmadena is during the spring and fall seasons when temperatures are warm and balmy without the humidity. But it is sultry and inviting all year long with plenty of sun-filled beaches and exciting places to see and visit. Wintertime is sometimes chilly and has a distinctly off-season feel to it. Many retirees live here during the off-season however to escape the cold northern European winters.

Sightseeing Highlights

Benalmadena Beaches

The beaches in Benalmadena are known for their beauty, peacefulness and moderate waves which lull you to bathe in the pleasant waters of the Mediterranean Ocean. The ocean follows the winding promenade of 9km from Puerto Marina (Benalmadena) to the village of Carvajal. Some beaches are known for their activities and sports and some are known for their quiet and serenity. The best times to swim in their waters is from May to early October as the rest of the year the water is somewhat chilly.

The beaches on the eastern side are somewhat larger in size with better facilities. The beaches on the west are quieter and are rockier so visitors tend to head for them when they want to fish or dive. Most of them are characterized by their dark sand, except three beaches – Malapesquera, Torrebermeja, and Santa Ana beaches – where the sand is fine and light colored. They are all accessible by foot or by car.

Fuengirola Beaches

Fuengirola has seven main beaches and they are all holders of the Blue Flag award. All the beaches have showers to wash off the salty water of the Mediterranean, designated areas for sports activities, and usually tranquil waters. The beaches are also equipped with lifeguards, sunbeds, umbrellas, beach front snack bars which offer food at reasonable prices, and of course, the promenade which lines the back of the beaches. There is a sign on every beach that marks the price of the umbrella and sunbed rentals which is usually 8 € for 2 beach beds and an umbrella.

Benalmádena Butterfly Park

Autovía del Mediterraneo A7, Salida 217
C/ Muérdago, s/n, El Retamar, Benalmádena 29639
 +34 951 211 196
http://www.mariposariodebenalmadena.com

The park's main building features a tropical garden made of glass to showcase the beauty of more than 1500 exotic butterflies.

Benalmádena Butterfly Park's main building is over 900 square meters and is 8 meters high. There are more than 150 different species of butterflies.

The garden is a unique experience where you can observe how these amazing creatures behave as they go through their life cycles. Witness how butterflies break out of their cocoons and take flight for the very first time. The life expectancy of a butterfly is just 2 weeks which means that every 14 days; the park renews its population automatically.

The park opens from 10am to 7pm every day. Admission is 9.50 € for adults, 6.50 € for children (3-12), and 7.50 € for retired and disabled guests.

Tivoli World Park

Av del Tivoli, s/n, 29631, Málaga
+34 952 57 70 16
http://www.tivoli.es/

Situated in Arroyo de la Miel, Tivoli World Park is the
Costa del Sol's most popular theme and Attraction Park.

It has many rides and attractions with restaurants, bars
and shows. With nice landscaped areas, this is a great
family day trip.

Tivoli World Park is divided into different sections
including the Andalusia section which has live Spanish
music and dancing, the Western Square, and Tivolilandia
which has rides for children.

The park is open until 2am in the summertime which
means you can go on all the rides at midnight when the
weather would be just about perfect. Here you can watch
authentic flamenco dancers, go to the theater or view
special exhibitions. If you want to take it easy you can just
stroll through the park and enjoy the great weather.

Take the cable car from the entrance of the park to the
peak of Mount Carramolo. Atop Mount Carramolo, you
can take in a glorious view of the Costa del Sol.

The entrance fee to the park is 7.95 €. Children under 1 meter in height will enter for free. You can also enquire about the Supertivolino Wristband, the Special CombiTicket, or the Special Offer MiniCombi for great deals. Opening and closing times differ by month so check their website before arrival.

Sealife Centre

Puerto Marina, s/n, 29630, Benalmádena
+34 952 56 01 50
http://www.visitsealife.com/benalmadena/#

At Sealife Center you can interact with the sea creatures in touch pools, learn fun facts which you will find across the aquarium, and view 36 spectacular displays. With over 2,000 creatures to watch you won't have a dull time here. The Sealife Center provides you with the chance to go up close and personal with some of these great creatures of the sea: sharks, seahorses, octopuses, eels, otters, tropical fish, and so many more.

Sealife Center has Europe's biggest collection of sharks in all of Europe. There is a walk-through called Lost City of Atlantis where you can stroll through a tunnel while looking at the many sea-life creatures swimming around you. Most of the exhibits and displays are indoors, but there is also an outside mini golf course, as well as a café where you can enjoy a cup of coffee while your kids play in the children's soft play area.

Admission is 16.25 € for adults (12-65), 14 € for children (3-11) and seniors (+65). If you would like a guide along your visit, there's a 3.95 € extra charge. Operating hours are from Monday through Sunday, 10am -6pm.

Selwo Marina

Parque de la Paloma, s/n 29630 Benalmádena
+34 902 19 04 82
http://www.selwomarina.es/

Situated behind Paloma Park in Benalmádena, this marine park is one of a kind. It is divided into the four areas of Antilles, La Hondonada, Amazonia, and Isla de Hielo. In the Antilles, you will be transported to the Caribbean where you will find a large Dolphinarium with bottlenose dolphins which you can see and interact with through the clear protective side panels of the saltwater pools. There is also an exhibition show there every day where the sea lions put on a show for your viewing pleasure.

La Hondonada (The Hollow) is an exotic bird exhibition which features birds from the Amazon in their natural habitat. You can see how magnificent these birds are with their amazingly rich colors and vibrant hues. Just a wooden bridge away is a play area for kids to discover and explore while they are having fun. Next to this area is a snack shop called Cabin of Delights where you can have your pick of snacks, refreshments, and ice-cream. The park has three other food kiosks/snack bars located in the park.

Amazonia is all about the Amazon region of Brazil. This amazing part of the park houses over 800 animals from over 50 species. You will find animals on land, in the trees, and in the water. Amazonia also has a place for ant nests with carefully reconstructed climate features that replicate those of the tropical jungle. Amazonia has over 40 species of plants and vegetation. As you walk through this part of the park, you find multimedia games, conservationist messages and reminders of the importance of taking care of our environment. The Amazon is one of the most celebrated and captivating areas on Earth.

Isla de Hielo (Ice Island), has a Penguinarium and features a large collection of penguins. You can visit the Meet the Penguins exhibit which will teach you all about these birds and their habitat. This part of the park also has educational games which act as a gentle reminder of what could happen to species like the Antarctic penguins if we don't start taking care of our environment.

There is also a cable car which you can take for a ride up to Calamorro Mountain.

Operating hours are from 10am to 6pm. Admission is 18.95 € for adults (10-65), 14.95 € for children (3-9) and senior citizens (+65). There are also entrance packs which will grant you access to the park as well as the cable car ride. This pack costs 25.70 € for adults and 19.90 € for children and seniors. If you want to make your visit to the park truly memorable, look into getting experience tickets which gets you entry tickets into the park as well as a chance to swim with your favorite ocean creature; dolphins, sea lions, or penguins. There are many choices and each experience is equally thrilling.

Plaza de la Constitucion

Located at the center of Fuengirola, the Plaza de la Constitucion has many stores, banks and bars. It also has cafés and coffee shops where you can relax and enjoy the charm and appeal of the town. If you take a walk through the narrow lanes of Fuengirola you will find an abundance of restaurants which offer local and international cuisine at moderate prices. And a 2 minute walk from the Church Square will take you to an area full of seafood restaurants aptly called Fish Alley. However you can find any type of food that you're in the mood for.

The Plaza's most famous attraction is the Church of Nuestra Senora del Rosario which was destroyed in the Spanish Civil War and rebuilt in 1946. One of the church's main features is its bronze doors and a striking mosaic of the Virgin Mary on the outside of the Church. It's also famous for is clock and bell tower whose chimes you can hear as you walk through the square. The church is still active today. Many people go for weddings, baptisms, and memorial services.

Fuengirola Zoo

Calle de Camilo José Cela, 6-8, Fuengirola
+34 952 66 63 01
http://www.bioparcfuengirola.es/en

This world-renowned zoo has many replicas of live animal habitats such as tropical forests, Asian and African jungles, farms, and many more. There are an abundance of animal species like crocodiles, Sumatran tigers, lemurs, bats, a myriad of birds and mammals, reptiles and amphibians. This zoo has won many awards for its beautiful architecture and layout and also for its help with the population of endangered animals by breeding them in captivity.

You are free to roam the zoo by yourself, or if you want to learn more about the zoo and its inhabitants, the zoo provides free guided visits with a specialist guide. There are also school visits, night time visits, and a special visit if you want to celebrate your birthday at the zoo. There's many fun things to do for your kids including a games area and a miniature farm. There are two restaurants – Africa Restaurant and Asia Café Shop – and a souvenir shop.

The zoo is a 10-minute walk from the Fuengirola town center. Admission is 17.90 € for adults, 12.50 € for children and seniors (+65). The zoo opens every day at 10am but closing times vary from month to month so please check the website before planning your visit.

Castle of Suhail

Castle of Suhail is located on top a hill 38m above sea level at the mouth of the Fuengirola River. It dates back to the middle of the 10th century when King Abdderraman III had it built to act as a defensive fortification. In the years that followed the castle was occupied by the Christians in the 1400s and by the French in the 1800s. Then in 1989, the castle was renovated and now it is used for cultural events, like the Festival Ciudad de Fuengirola.

This castle is one of the most interesting buildings in Fuengirola. Inside, there is a museum which carries exhibits on the various attributes of the castle. Opening hours at the castle are from 10am to 2pm and from 6pm to 9pm. The building closes on Mondays.

Fuengirola Museum

This museum first opened its doors in 2003. It is located in the heart of Fuengirola at Calle Maria Josefa Larrucea. The museum houses artifacts from Roman and Arab times. It also contains statues and figurines, like the statue of the Venus of Fuengirola which is a white marble statue that dates back to the Roman era. On display are informational texts about the culture of the town and its history. The museum's operating hours are from 10am to 2pm. Admission is 2 € for adults and 1.5 € for children and seniors, children younger than 10 years old can enter for free.

Aquapark

Carretera Nacional 340 km.209, Mijas Costa, 29640
Fuengirola
+34 95 246 0404
http://www.aquamijas.com/en/#!/

This water park should be on your list of places to see in
Fuengirola, especially if you're travelling with kids. On
the outskirts of Fuengirola, this exhilarating water park is
open from April to September. The park features thrilling
water rides, adventures and lots of sunshine. There are
slides that whirl around several times before you get to
the pool and there are slides that just throw you into the
water in a straight line.

Besides the wet and slippery rides and slides, there is a
wave pool, water aerobics, beach areas, and a whole lot
more. There are also shows with dancing and live music,
a massage area and spa treatments if you'd like to take a
break from the water.

If you want to take a break from all the zipping and
sliding, take a stroll to the restaurant and bar where you
can relax and cool off. The restaurant and bar offer
delicious food and snacks. However, it is advisable to
take a cool box with a picnic and drinks as the park can be
quite costly.

The park opens daily from the first week in May at 10:30am and closes at either 5:30pm, 6pm, or 7pm depending on the month. If you go after 2:30 in the afternoon, you can get a 30% discount on your ticket. Admission is 23 € for adults, 17 € for children ages 8-12, 12 € for children ages 3-7, and 15 € for seniors. There is a family ticket which you can buy for 58 € which includes 2 adults and 2 kids ages 3-7.

Arab Baths

Avenida de Mar 4-6, Benalmadena Costa
Costa del Sol 29630
952-444 660
http://www.aguadeoriente.com/html/english/aguadeoriente.html

The locals refer to the Arab Baths as Agua de Oriente and is a perfect place for relaxation and indulgence. It is located next to Puerto Marina in Benalmadena but when you visit the Baths you will be transported to another time and place. The Baths feature scented candles and oils, water gently cascading from a fountain, and candles softly glowing. The Baths, or small pools, have different temperatures. The first one you start out with is at 33C then you move on to the pool with the 38C temperature, then back into the first pool. Finally, you go into the colder pool called Firgidarium which is 17C but for only a few moments. These Baths energize you and wake up the circulatory system giving you a revitalized feeling.

If that isn't enough you can treat yourself to an invigorating body massage, a Turkish Sauna and have a sip from a collection of exotic teas located in the relaxation room. You can treat yourself to only the bath at 27 €, a bath with massage which can last 15 minutes, 30 minutes, or 45 minutes at 41 €, 53 € and 74 € respectively. The Baths are open daily and you should call beforehand to reserve your session which can be at these times: 10-11:30am, 12-1:30pm, 2-3:30pm, 4-5:30pm, 6-7:30pm, 8-9:30pm and 10-11:30pm.

Parque de la Paloma

Avenida Garcia Lorca s/n; 29631, 29631 Benalmádena
http://benalmadenapueblo.com/place/paloma-park-arroyo-de-la-miel/

Paloma Park is located on 200,000 square miles of luscious greenery in the center of Arroyo de la Miel, the economic zone of Benalmadena. This is one of the most impressive and most visited parks on the Costa del Sol. it features a wide range of animal species such as fish, turtles, ducks, roosters, rabbits, sheep, and peacocks. You can feed bread to some of the animals. You can hire a bicycle to ride across the beautiful grounds of the park. There is also a library, 3 cafes, a fountain and several streams which add magic to this charming place. For the children in your group, there are 2 safely-equipped playgrounds and play areas. There is also a Cactus Garden with more than 450 species of cacti. The amount of greenery is huge and wonderful for just sitting and relaxing, having a picnic, or playing games.

You can find most of the fish, ducks, swans, etc. swimming merrily in the large artificial lake found in the center of the park. There is a quadricycle which you can rent for a fun ride around the lake. It seats 4 adults. The rest of the animals you'll spot running around will delight young and old alike! The big, unpredictable animals like ostriches and mountain goats are kept in a closed area for your safety and theirs.

The park is open from 9am to 10pm during the winter months and until 11pm during the summer months.

Roman Ruins

Various Locations

The first mention of the city of Fuengirola dates back to the 2nd century BC. There have been archaeological artifacts and remains which were unearthed over the years. For example, there was a sculpture called the Venus of Fuengirola which is now on display at the History Museum. The remains of a Roman town called Seul have been found in the area next to the castle. There is another very interesting historical site called *Finca del Secretario* (The Secretary's Estate). On the promenade at Los Boliches beach there are Roman pillars still standing today which were discovered in 1984.

Mijas

Taking a 20-minute bus ride to the village of Mijas will be an unforgettable trip and is one of the sightseeing highlights of this area. You can walk through the picturesque streets of this hill town which retain their ancient and charming feel. The streets of the historic old quarter have a uniquely Moorish feel to them, and many buildings and monuments are of historical significance. If you want to take advantage of the mountains, you can take a hike up the hills of the Sierra de Mijas and enjoy the wonderful weather as you gaze over the Mediterranean in the distance and Mijas Costa and Fuengirola below. If you enjoy playing golf, there are fine courses located at various parts of Mijas.

Recommendations for the Budget Traveller

Places to Stay

Aparthotel Veramar

C/ Burgos, 2 Fuengirola 29640
+34 607 51 28 28
www.aparthotelveramar.com/

This intimate aparthotel is rated at 3 stars and is located near the castle in Fuengirola.

It is only a few minutes away from the hustle and bustle of downtown and the relaxing beaches and only a 30-minute ride to Malaga airport.

The hotel offers a full set of facilities and services that will ensure you have a satisfying and wonderful stay. Some of its top-quality amenities include satellite TV, microwave, fridge, heating, telephone and a balcony or terrace. The apartments also offers an onsite swimming pool, bar, TV room, and a restaurant which serves a delicious array of tantalizing dishes.

Ronda 4 Apartments

Paseo Marítimo Rey de España, 96 29640 Fuengirola
+34 952 66 07 16
http://www.apartamentosronda4.com/es

The Ronda 4 apartments are a terrific choice for those who love being only a stone's throw away from the beach. All you have to do to get to the beach is walk across the promenade and you're there.

You can also enjoy the many shops, bars, and restaurants that line the promenade with its beautiful palm trees and comfortable benches. On the grounds of the apartments, you will find a swimming pool with a section for children and a pool-side bar for snacks and refreshment.

Each apartment comes with kitchen facilities, a telephone, a TV, a refrigerator and much more. The apartments are clean and well-furnished and the prices average at about 18 € for a one room apartment.

Fuengirola Beach

Av de la Encarnación, 2, 29640 Fuengirola, Málaga
+34 951 06 27 00
http://www.fuengirolabeach.com/

If you're visiting Fuengirola with your family or your partner, this hotel is perfect for you.

It is a short walk from the exhilarating beaches and the exciting attractions. Open since 2001, it's a 3-star apartment-hotel with your choice of one bedroom or two. There are two swimming pools that have a separate section for children, an arena for multi-sports for playing tennis, volleyball and basketball. There is a sun terrace, a bar/lounge, two restaurants and three bars. If there are children in your group, there is also a large playground.

All rooms feature a kitchenette, a lounge area with extra sofa beds, satellite TV, phone, safe, balcony or terrace. The apartments are spacious and well-furnished. Prices are about 18 € for a one bedroom apartment which can accommodate up to 4 people.

Hotel Reyesol

Calle Marbella, 41, 29640 Fuengirola
+34 952 47 37 04

Opened in 2009, this hotel has well-furnished rooms, affordable accommodations and is just minutes away from the beach and all the thrilling attractions at Fuengirola such as Tivoli Amusement Park, or enjoy the warm weather and take time off for a game of golf which can be found in leisure centers in the area. If you'd like a dip in the pool, both indoor and outdoor, then these leisure centers have that too since there is no pool on the hotel grounds.

Hotel Reyesol is situated next to the Fuengirola Town Hall and less than 200m to the nearest beach area. It features a complimentary breakfast, excellent coffee shop, Wi-Fi, and so much more. Each room comes with a balcony or a terrace and a lot of contemporary and indispensable amenities to make your stay comfortable and pleasant. Prices are from 23 €.

Club La Costa Marina Del Sol

Urb. Marina del Sol, Ctra. de Cadiz km 206
Mijas Costa 29649
0800-009-6070
http://www.clcworld.com/costadelsol/club-la-costa-costa-del-sol

Club La Costa Marina Del Sol was built in the Andalusian style. The fantastic architecture and the beautiful gardens are what make this hotel so special.

There are six swimming pools on the hotel grounds, one is heated for those winter months and one is designed specifically for children.

The hotel is just a short walk away from the beautiful beaches of Fuengirola and it is only 1.5km from the town center. The restaurants onsite offer exquisite cuisine with fresh, succulent dishes both local and international. There is also a bar where you can order coffee, light snacks, or enjoy a soothing cocktail. The rooms are well furnished and come with satellite TV, kitchen, washing machine, hair dryer, a safe, a DVD player, a phone, and a balcony or terrace so you can take in the wonderful view of the coastline and the sapphire-blue Mediterranean waters. Prices start at 31€ for a studio.

Places to Eat & Drink

The Lounge at Pinoccios

Avda Antonio Machado 57, Conjunto Las Gaviotas, 31-32, 29630 Benalmadena
+34 952 561 989
http://www.pinocciosbar.com/index.html

Pinoccios features everything from light bites to evening meals to traditional Spanish Tapas, and there is also a Breakfast menu.

There many vegetarian dishes and delicious desserts that will make your taste buds sing. The restaurant has a lounge bar, terrace (which can hold up to 50 people) and an inside dining room. Pinoccios specializes in Thai Fish Cakes, Black Pudding with mustard sauce and cheesecake just to name a few. The prices are in the range of 2-19 € and are great value for money.

Restaurante Hermanos Perea

Paseo Marítimo Rey de España, 28, Playa Carvajal, Fuengirola
+34 952 661 226

This is a bar and a restaurant in one. It specializes in skewers, cane fish and fresh fish. It has an excellent view of the Mediterranean as it is by the beach. With prices ranging between 10 and 20 €, you are guaranteed a great value for your money.

Antonio Videra

Paseo Marítimo Los Boliches, Fuengirola
+34 952 119 193
www.antoniovidera.com/

This beachfront restaurant opened in the 1970s and has been one of the most popular beach restaurants ever since. The restaurant has a cozy inner dining area as well as an airy seaside terrace. It specializes in seafood as well as various meat dishes, pasta, and tasty deserts. Prices are between 10 and 20 €.

Jacks

La Darsena Levanter Local C5-6, 29630, Puerto
Marina, Benalmadena
+34 952 563 673
http://www.jacksamericanbrasserie.com/jacks-
american-brasserie-puerto-banus-costa-del-sol-hours-
directions

This restaurant offers American food that is classical and
mouth-watering.

The ambience is relaxed and laid-back. It is located in
Puerto Marina and can cater to private events and
birthday parties as well. *Jacks* offers the best in all-time
family favorites with fresh ingredients. There is also a
kids' menu with chicken fingers, fish fingers, hot dog, or
burger all which come with their own order of fries, or
salad. Prices range between 15 and 20 €.

Sakura

Darsena de Levante, Puerto Marina, Benalmadena
+34 952 964195

Sakura is a restaurant that offers Japanese cuisine and
other types of Asian food. There are several set menus to
choose from. It is located in the beautiful Puerto Marina
and you will unobstructed view of the marina and the
shimmering Mediterranean. This restaurant opens its
doors from 12pm until 12am so you can enjoy the
picturesque panorama during the day and night.

Places to Shop

El Corte Ingles

Avenida Nuestro Padre Jesus, Cautivo, 33, 29640, Fuengirola
+34 952 19 86 80
www.elcorteingles.es/

This large shopping center is a 10-minute walk from the Fuengirola Town Center. It offers top quality shops and boutiques for your shopping pleasure. El Corte Ingles is the most famous shopping chain in Spain. If you're not in the mood for walking and would like to go by bus, there's a free courtesy bus that leaves the Town Center for the shopping center on a regular basis. The operating hours for El Corte Ingles is from 9:30am to 9:30pm daily, except on Sundays when they're closed.

Miramar Shopping & Leisure Centre

Avenida Encarnación, 29640, Fuengirola
+34 952 19 81 95
http://www.parquemiramar.com/

This shopping centre is located next to Suhail Castle and here you will find everything from jewelry to clothing.

There is a fresh produce market where you will find the freshest and tastiest local food. Miramar Shopping and Leisure Centre has a cinema complex if you want time away from the beach. Operating hours at the shopping center are from 10am until 10pm except on Sundays when they're closed.

Skates & Bikes Shop

Av. Miramar 1, Edificio Miramar Bog 7-5 Local 1 C.P 29640, Fuengirola
+34 951 407 428
http://www.sbsshop.es/

This is one of the best shops to visit if you like BMX bikes, scooters and skating and everything you might need to accessorize your ride. This shop also has some of the best-known name brands and some not so well known.

Fuengirola Market

This market holds a fair on a weekly basis which includes a flea market where you can go hunting for bargains while enjoying the beautiful weather and surroundings. It runs every Tuesday and is considered to be one of the largest open-air markets on the Costa de Sol. it's a great attraction for both tourists and locals because of the ample assortment of goods on sale there. It is held in the mid-section of Fuengirola.

On Saturdays and Sundays you will find similar second-hand markets at the far end of Fuengirola next to the castle hill. If you're there in October, make sure to check out the Rosario Fair which lasts about a week. It is held in honor of the town's Patroness, Our Lady of the Rosary. There is usually a parade of horsemen as well as singing and dancing, competitions and prizes, and other great activities for you to enjoy. It's held in the same venue as the weekly Tuesday market.

Printed in Great Britain
by Amazon

41012614R00046